Essential Question
What impact do our actions have on our world?

Marjory Stoneman Douglas

GUARDIAN OF THE EVERGLADES

BY JANE KELLEY

Digital Vision/Punchstock

Introduction

The Everglades in southern Florida were named because the glades, or grassy places, seemed to go on forever. Water flowed all across the area, too. Many people looked at this **landscape** and saw a **useless** swamp. The ground was too wet for growing crops or building houses.

Writer Marjory Stoneman Douglas felt differently. She could see that the Everglades area was special. She described the beauty of the Everglades: "The miracle of the light pours over the green and brown expanse of saw grass and of water, shining and slow-moving below."

This area in the Everglades is called a freshwater prairie.

MedioImages/PunchStock

CHAPTER ONE
Early Life

Douglas's writings about the Everglades **influenced** many people. But how did she end up writing about the Everglades? She never spent a lot of time outdoors. She wasn't from Florida.

Marjory was born on April 7, 1890 in Minneapolis. She lived in Massachusetts for most of her childhood. Marjory liked to spend time in libraries, and she loved learning new things from books. This is how she started learning how to do research—a skill she needed when she became a writer.

This is a photograph of Marjory when she was one and a half years old.

Marjory went to Wellesley College. In her senior year, she was editor of the college yearbook. She was also the class **orator** because she was very good at giving speeches.

Marjory attended Wellesley College in Massachusetts.

After she graduated in 1912, Marjory didn't know what to do next. Back then, women were not encouraged to have careers. So Marjory worked in a department store. She taught grammar and math to the sales clerks.

Marjory married Kenneth Douglas in 1914. When her marriage ended in 1915, she moved to Miami, Florida, where her father lived.

Douglas's father, Frank Stoneman, was the editor of *The Miami Herald*. He hired his daughter to write the newspaper's society column. Douglas was excited to be writing. Her father told her that he wanted to save an area near the city called the Everglades.

Douglas's father had a passion for saving Miami's old neighborhoods.

When World War I started, Douglas joined the Red Cross. The Red Cross helped people who were suffering because of the war. Douglas was sent to Europe. She wrote about the work the Red Cross was doing in Europe and **urged** people to support these efforts. She also saw the **plight** of refugees who had to leave their homes during the war. As a result, Douglas was always sympathetic to people in trouble.

World War I ended in 1918. When Douglas came back to Miami in 1920, the city had four times as many people as before. The city needed more land. But a lot of the land was part of the Everglades. **Developers** dug canals to drain the **wetlands**. They didn't think about the **native** animals and plants that lived there.

Douglas became *The Miami Herald*'s assistant editor. She wrote a column about important **issues**, such as good living conditions and women's rights. She also urged that the Everglades should be made a national park. This would protect the area.

Draining the wetlands affected the animals and plants that lived there.

(bc) Galen Rowell/CORBIS, (b) Wetzel and Company/Janice McDonald

STOP AND CHECK

What are some of the issues Douglas wrote about?

CHAPTER TWO

A River of Grass

Douglas worked hard at the newspaper. She also started **campaigns** to help people, such as providing milk for poor families.

This great egret lives in the Everglades.

In 1924, Douglas quit her job at the newspaper. She decided to write short stories instead. She sold her stories to magazines. Although Douglas didn't work at the newspaper anymore, she never forgot the social issues that were important to her.

Douglas couldn't always sell her work. Sometimes it was hard for her to earn a living.

Then in 1941, her friend Hervey Allen asked her to write a book about the Miami River.

Douglas didn't want to write about the Miami River. She wanted to write a book about the Everglades. Allen agreed to publish the book.

Douglas interviewed people about the area. She wrote about topics ranging from the Native Americans who lived there to the **geology** of the Everglades.

Native Americans rowed through the Everglades in canoes.

Then Douglas came up with a new way to describe the Everglades. It changed how people thought. She called the Everglades a **glistening** "river of grass."

In her book, Douglas said the Everglades were unlike any other place in the world:

> They are ... one of the **unique** regions of the earth, **remote**, never wholly known. Nothing anywhere else is like them; their vast glittering openness, wider than the enormous visible round of the horizon, the racing free saltness and sweetness of their massive winds, under the dazzling blue heights of space.

What makes the Everglades unique? Look at the lake on the map. Water flows south from the lake across limestone. Sawgrass grows on top of the stone. This kind of water flow isn't found anywhere else.

Douglas was right: The Everglades really are a river of grass.

THE ECOSYSTEM

The Everglades have many different habitats. Each habitat is home to a group of living things that depend on each other and the environment. These habitats form the Everglades ecosystem.

If the temperature isn't right, or there isn't enough food or water, then the ecosystem could collapse.

WATER FLOW THROUGH THE EVERGLADES

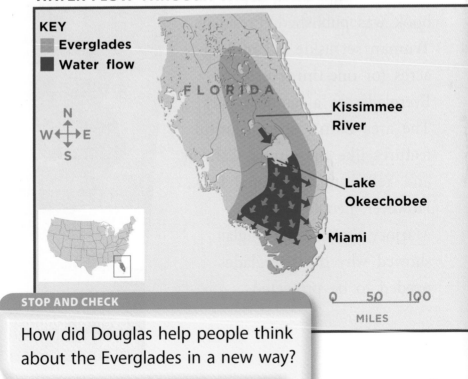

KEY
- Everglades
- Water flow

FLORIDA

N
W E
S

Kissimmee River

Lake Okeechobee

• Miami

0   50   100
MILES

STOP AND CHECK

How did Douglas help people think about the Everglades in a new way?

CHAPTER THREE

Fighting On

The Everglades: River of Grass was published in 1947. It sold 7,500 copies in one month. People liked the way Douglas described the Everglades. She explained how people were connected to this special place. The Everglades provided water for people. If they were drained, water wouldn't flow into the **aquifers** under the sawgrass. Southern Florida would become a desert.

One month after her book was published, President Truman set aside 1.5 million acres (or one-third) of the Everglades as a national park. The area didn't have beautiful features like the Grand Canyon and Yellowstone National Park. However, people such as Marjory Stoneman Douglas showed why the Everglades needed to be protected.

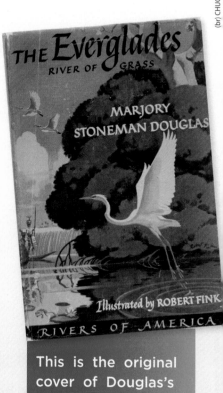

This is the original cover of Douglas's book.

Douglas was in awe of the Everglades. However, she thought it was a difficult landscape. She said, "... it's too buggy, too wet, too generally inhospitable."

Douglas also wrote other nonfiction books about Florida. Two of these books, *Freedom River* and *Alligator Crossing,* were for children.

She continued to speak about her most famous book. Some parts of the Everglades were protected by the national park, but the rest was still at risk. The owners of sugar **plantations** wanted to control the water so they could grow more sugarcane. Developers wanted more land to build houses. So canals were dug. Water was drained from the marshes.

Douglas played an important role in saving the Florida Everglades.

STOP AND CHECK

How are the Everglades different from other national parks?

In 1969, developers wanted to build an airport in the Everglades. Joe Browder was a TV reporter and an **environmentalist**. He asked Douglas to help him stop the airport. So Douglas started a group called Friends of the Everglades and spoke out against the airport project.

People listened, and the airport wasn't built. However, Douglas said that water in the Everglades was still a problem. Something had to be done to **restore** it. She wanted polluters to clean up the water. Douglas also wanted to get rid of the canals that carried water away from the area.

PROTECTING OTHER WETLANDS

People around the world are working to protect special places in their communities. In 1990, Rosa Hilda Ramos formed Communities United Against Contamination. The group is in San Juan, Puerto Rico.

The group got companies to clean up pollution and pay fines. The money from fines was used to buy Las Cucharillas Marsh. Now this wetland is a safe place for birds and people.

(bc) Photo courtesy Goldman Environmental Prize, (b) Wetzel and Company/Janice McDonald

This bird is hunting for food in Las Cucharillas Marsh.

Douglas kept fighting. When she was in her 90s, developers threatened the Everglades again. So Douglas spoke out again.

Sam Poole, from the South Florida Water Management District, said, "One small person can make a difference. She made a huge difference."

Douglas received many awards, such as the Medal of Freedom. The award said that her work "**enhanced** our nation's respect for our precious environment." Her work really did improve the way people thought about the natural world.

STOP AND CHECK

What did the Everglades need to be protected from?

President Clinton gave Douglas the Medal of Freedom.

Conclusion

Douglas wanted to save the plants and animals that live in the Everglades.

The Everglades Forever Act was passed in Florida in 1994. The purpose of the law was to preserve and restore the water in the Everglades.

Douglas knew that making laws wasn't enough to protect the Everglades. People needed to care about protecting this special place. So she **founded** the Young Friends of the Everglades. Douglas said she started this group to "Take the children out to the Glades and let them learn. Education will be the only way to save the Glades."

In 1997, 1.3 million acres of the Everglades were named the Marjory Stoneman Douglas Wilderness. Douglas died in 1998, when she was 108. Her work still inspires anyone who wants to make a difference in the world.

Respond to Reading

Summarize

Use important details to summarize the biography of Marjory Stoneman Douglas. Your graphic organizer may help you.

Problem	Solution

Text Evidence

1. Reread page 10. Why did Douglas think that draining the wetlands was a problem? How did she think the problem could be solved? **PROBLEM AND SOLUTION**

2. Look at the word *sympathetic* on page 5. Use clues in the paragraph to figure out what it means. **VOCABULARY**

3. Write about how Douglas helped the Everglades. Give examples of the problems she faced and the actions she took to solve them. **WRITE ABOUT READING**

Compare Texts
Read about a schoolgirl who took action
by planting trees.

The Story of the
Tree Musketeers

In 1987, there was a drought in California. Tara Church was eight years old, and her scout troop was going camping. Tara's mom asked the girls to choose between paper and tin plates. Paper plates didn't need to be washed, so they would save water. However, paper comes from trees, so tin plates would save trees. The girls decided to plant more trees.

Tin camping plates save trees. Campers can also reduce waste by reusing utensils.

(bkgd) Keith Levit/Design Pics, (br) JoeFox/Alamy

Trees are an important resource. Tree roots help soil stay in place. Trees make oxygen and help clean the air. They provide food and shelter for other living things. The leaves provide shade, which keeps cities cooler in hot weather.

Tara and her friends planted their first tree in El Segundo, California. They named it Marcie the Marvelous Tree.

The children planted more trees and asked other scout groups to do the same. They called themselves the Tree Musketeers after the book *The Three Musketeers*.

Their organization grew. Kids taught other kids how to help the environment. Kids learned how to plant trees and take care of them, and how to get more kids to take part.

In 1988, the Tree Musketeers went to Washington, D.C. to receive an environmental youth award.

The work of the Tree Musketeers was ready to **export** to other countries. The group began to share ideas with people all over the world. Their efforts got many more kids working to help the environment.

Today, the group has projects such as the One in a Million tree-planting program and Partners for the Planet. These projects encourage kids to protect nature.

Marcie the Marvelous Tree is more than 50 feet tall now. The tree is still helping to cool the city and clean the air. And it still inspires kids to make a difference.

Planting trees is an easy way for kids to help the environment in their communities.

(bkgd) Keith Levit/Design Pics, (br) Jeremy Woodhouse/Blend Images/AGE Fotostock

Make Connections

Why do you think Tara's ideas have spread so far around the world? ESSENTIAL QUESTION

Compare Marjory Stoneman Douglas with Tara in *The Story of the Tree Musketeers*. How are they alike? How are they different? TEXT TO TEXT

Glossary

aquifers *(A-kwuh-fuhrz)* layers of soil or rock that can store water *(page 10)*

campaigns *(kam-PAYNZ)* organized actions to bring about change *(page 7)*

developers *(di-VEL-uh-puhrz)* business people that build houses or other structures *(page 6)*

environmentalist *(in-vigh-ruhn-MEN-tuhl-ist)* a person who helps protect the environment *(page 12)*

geology *(jee-AH-luh-jee)* the rocks and other materials that make up Earth *(page 8)*

wetlands *(WET-landz)* areas soaked with water, such as swamps *(page 6)*

Index

Focus on Science

Purpose To learn about threats to your local environment and to take action

Procedure

Step 1 With a partner or group, research local environmental problems. Some examples of problems are getting people to recycle, or cleaning up a trash-filled park.

Step 2 Choose a problem you would like to help with. Check with your teacher to make sure it's not dangerous. Identify the cause or causes of the problem. Think of something people could do to help, such as removing trash.

Step 3 With the help of your teacher and other adults, plan a work day at the site. What supplies will you need? How will you let people in your community know what you're doing?

Step 4 After your work day, report back to the class. What did you do? Was the work day a success? Why or why not?

Conclusion How did your actions improve the environment? What else needs to be done?